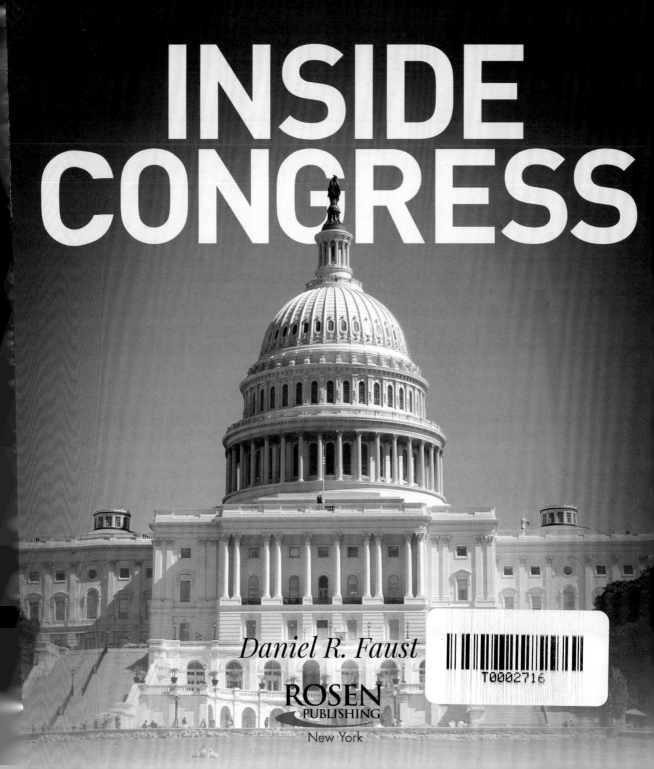

# ROSEN ✔ *Verified*
## U.S. GOVERNMENT

# INSIDE CONGRESS

Daniel R. Faust

**ROSEN**
PUBLISHING
New York

Published in 2021 by The Rosen Publishing Group, Inc.
29 East 21st Street, New York, NY 10010

First Edition

Editor: Siyavush Saidian
Book Design: Reann Nye

Photo Credits: Cover Dominic Labbe/Momnet/Getty Images; series Art PinkPueblo/Shutterstock.com; p. 5 SergiyN/Shutterstock.com; p. 7 David Smart/Shutterstock.com; pp. 8–9 https://commons.wikimedia.org/wiki/File:Scene_at_the_Signing_of_the_Constitution_of_the_United_States.jpg; p. 10 Orhan Cam/Shutterstock.com; p. 11 Photo 12/Universal Images Group/Getty Images; pp. 12–13 Mike Albright Photography/Shutterstock.com; p. 14 Sarah Silbiger/Getty Images News/Getty Images; pp. 16–17 mark reinstein/Shutterstock.com; p. 19 YES Market Media/Shutterstock.com; p. 21 MCT/ Tribune News Service/Getty Images; p. 23 Morphart Creation/Shutterstock.com; p. 25 Tom Williams/CQ-Roll Call, Inc./Getty Images News/Getty Images; p. 27 (Seal of the Vice President of the United States) https://commons.wikimedia.org/wiki/File:Seal_of_the_Vice_President_of_the_United_States.svg; p. 27 (Seal of the Speaker of the US House of Representatives) https://commons.wikimedia.org/wiki/File:Seal_of_the_Speaker_of_the_US_House_of_Representatives.svg; p. 27 (President Pro Tempore US Senate Seal) https://commons.wikimedia.org/wiki/File:President_Pro_Tempore_US_Senate_Seal.svg; p. 27 (Seal of the United States Secretary of State) https://commons.wikimedia.org/wiki/File:Seal_of_the_United_States_Secretary_of_State.svg; p. 29 Katherine Welles/Shutterstock.com; p. 30 Getty Images/Getty Images News/Getty Images; p. 31 MANDEL NGAN/AFP/Getty Images; p. 32 Daniel Jedzura/Shutterstock.com; p. 34 Rob Crandall/Shutterstock.com; p. 35 Mega Pixel/Shutterstock.com; p. 37 Bettmann/Getty Images; p. 39 Jana Shea/Shutterstock.com; p. 41 Orhan Cam/Shutterstock.com; p. 42 https://en.wikipedia.org/wiki/File:Richard_Nixon_presidential_portrait.jpg; p. 43 (Johnson) https://commons.wikimedia.org/wiki/File:Andrew_Johnson_photo_portrait_head_and_shoulders,_c1870-1880-Edit1.jpg; p. 43 (Clinton) https://commons.wikimedia.org/wiki/File:Bill_Clinton.jpg; p. 43 (Trump) https://en.wikipedia.org/wiki/File:Donald_Trump_official_portrait.jpg; p. 45 SAUL LOEB/AFp/Getty Images.

Library of Congress Cataloging-in-Publication Data

Names: Faust, Daniel R., author.
Title: Inside Congress / Daniel R. Faust.
Description: New York : Rosen Publishing, 2021. | Series: Rosen verified:
   U.S. government | Includes index.
Identifiers: LCCN 2020005122 | ISBN 9781499468618 (library binding) | ISBN
   9781499468601 (paperback)
Subjects: LCSH: United States. Congress—Juvenile literature. |
   Legislation—United States—Juvenile literature.
Classification: LCC JK1025 .F38 2021 | DDC 328.73—dc23
LC record available at https://lccn.loc.gov/2020005122

Manufactured in the United States of America

CPSIA Compliance Information: Batch #BSR20. For Further Information contact Rosen Publishing, New York, New York at 1-800-237-9932.

Find us on

# CONTENTS

# THE LEGISLATIVE BRANCH

Have you ever stopped to think about why you need to pay taxes? Or why you need to be 18 to vote? Many of the laws that tell us what we can and can't do are created by the **federal** government. Our government is made up of three branches. The three branches are the executive branch, legislative branch, and judicial branch. Each branch has its own job.

The legislative branch is also called Congress. Congress makes the laws we all follow. The executive branch is run by the president. It makes sure that these laws are followed. The U.S. Supreme Court is part of the judicial branch. It decides if any of these laws go against the U.S. Constitution.

The president of the United States leads the country, but they're just one part of the federal government system.

# SETTING UP CONGRESS

The three branches of government were **established** by the U.S. Constitution. This document has sections that explain the job of each branch. These sections are called articles. The U.S. Congress is set up in Article I of the Constitution.

Article I created the two houses of Congress. The two houses are the Senate and the House of Representatives. Each house has different powers, but they both work together to make laws.

## THE SEVEN ARTICLES OF THE U.S. CONSTITUTION

- Article I created the U.S. Congress.
- Article II created the office of the president.
- Article III created the Supreme Court.
- Article IV defines the relationship between the federal government and the states.
- Article V gives Congress the ability to change, or amend, the Constitution.
- Article VI states that the Constitution is "the law of the land."
- Article VII explained how the Constitution could become law.

The U.S. Constitution is a living document. This means it can be changed and updated.

*We the People*

insure domestic Tranquility, provide for the common

and our Posterity, do ordain and establish this Constitu

Section 1. All legislative Powe

## THE U.S. CONSTITUTION

The U.S. Constitution is the basis of the government and basic laws of the United States. It also includes the Bill of Rights. The Bill of Rights gives all U.S. citizens certain basic rights, such as freedom of speech.

# THE ARTICLES OF CONFEDERATION

The U.S. Constitution was not America's first constitution. After winning the American Revolution, the Founding Fathers wrote the Articles of Confederation. The new states wanted to remain **independent**, so the Articles of Confederation created a weak federal government. It had only one branch. The only branch in the new government was the Congress of the Confederation.

This new government didn't work. The country needed something stronger. The Founding Fathers came together again and wrote the U.S. Constitution.

The Constitutional Convention took place between May and September 1787. Instead of adjusting the Articles of Confederation, the members ended up creating the U.S. Constitution.

# THE TWO HOUSES

The U.S. Constitution created a Congress with two houses, or chambers. This is called a bicameral legislature. The word "bicameral" means "two houses." The two houses of the U.S. Congress are the Senate and the House of Representatives. The American people elect the men and women who serve in Congress. The two houses work together to pass laws.

The U.S. Capitol is one of the most recognizable buildings in Washington, D.C. Both the Senate and the House of Representatives have offices and meeting rooms there.

### THE NEW JERSEY PLAN

The New Jersey Plan was one suggestion on how the country would be governed. This plan would give every state the same number of votes in Congress.

### THE VIRGINIA PLAN

The Virginia Plan called for a Congress with two houses. The number of members in each house would be based on the state's population.

### THE GREAT COMPROMISE

The Great Compromise combined the New Jersey Plan and the Virginia Plan. The Great Compromise created a Congress with two houses. One house would be based on a state's population. The other house would give each state the same number of votes.

# THE ELASTIC CLAUSE

The Constitution gives the U.S. Congress many important powers. Congress is allowed to make laws, raise an army, declare war, collect taxes, and decide how the government will spend the money it collects. Congress can also investigate the actions of government employees and **agencies**.

There is a special section of the Constitution called the elastic clause. This lets Congress make any new law it needs to make to do its job.

Because they directly represent the people, many senators and representatives hold town hall meetings. These meetings are a chance for people to speak to their representatives in person.

# WHO CAN RUN FOR CONGRESS?

The Constitution sets up the rules stating who can and cannot serve in each house of Congress.

## HOUSE OF REPRESENTATIVES

- Must be at least 25 years old
- Must have been a U.S. citizen for at least seven years
- Must live in the state they represent

## SENATE

- Must be at least 30 years old
- Must have been a U.S. citizen for at least nine years
- Must live in the state they represent

# THE HOUSE OF REPRESENTATIVES

One of the chambers of the U.S. Congress is the House of Representatives. It's sometimes called the lower house of Congress. Like the U.S. Senate, the House of Representatives was established by Article I of the Constitution.

The House of Representatives has 435 members. Each state elects a certain number of representatives. The number of representatives elected by each state is based on that state's population.

The leader of the House of Representatives is known as the Speaker of the House. In January 2019, the Democratic majority elected Nancy Pelosi as Speaker of the House.

# REPRESENTATION IN NUMBERS

Each state elects a different number of representatives to the House of Representatives. States with more people, like California or New York, have more members. States with fewer people, like Alaska or Delaware, have fewer members. Representatives are elected every two years. Below is a chart of the states with the most members and the states with the fewest members.

| STATES WITH THE MOST REPRESENTATIVES | | STATES WITH THE LEAST REPRESENTATIVES | |
|---|---|---|---|
| CALIFORNIA | 53 | ALASKA | 1 |
| TEXAS | 36 | DELAWARE | 1 |
| NEW YORK | 27 | MONTANA | 1 |
| FLORIDA | 27 | NORTH DAKOTA | 1 |
| ILLINOIS | 18 | SOUTH DAKOTA | 1 |
| PENNSYLVANIA | 18 | VERMONT | 1 |
| OHIO | 16 | WYOMING | 1 |

## ✔ VERIFIED

You can learn more about the members and history of the House of Representatives on its official website:
**https://www.house.gov**

# THE POWERS OF THE HOUSE

Both houses of Congress help to make the country's laws. Members of the House of Representatives can **propose** new laws. They also vote on a law proposed by someone else. The House of Representatives has the power to create laws that raise money for the government. These laws are called taxes.

The House of Representatives can punish or remove members who misbehave. The House also has the power of impeachment. An impeachment is a criminal charge against a government **official**.

Although there are no assigned seats in the House of Representatives, Democrats sit on the left side of the center aisle and Republicans sit on the right side of the center aisle.

17

# THE SENATE

The second chamber of the U.S. Congress is called the Senate. It's sometimes called the upper house of Congress. Each state has the same number of senators. There are a total of 100 senators in the U.S. Senate. Each state elects two senators.

A senator serves for a **term** of six years. After those six years, the senator must be reelected. Every two years, about one-third of the Senate is running for reelection.

## TIEBREAKER

Because there is an even number of senators, it's possible that some votes might end in a tie. In the case of a tie, the vice president of the United States is called on to cast the tiebreaking vote.

## ✓ VERIFIED

The Senate's official website is full of information about its members, committees, and ongoing debates: **https://www.senate.gov**

According to the Constitution, the vice president of the United States also serves as the president of the Senate. Vice President Mike Pence became president of the Senate in January 2017.

# THE POWERS OF THE SENATE

Like the House of Representatives, the members of the Senate can propose new laws. The Senate can punish or remove senators. The Senate also has some unique powers.

The Senate has the power to confirm or **deny** presidential appointments. The Senate holds a trial for anyone who has been impeached by the House. The Senate also has the power to ratify, or approve, a treaty with a foreign nation.

## PRESIDENTIAL APPOINTMENTS

The U.S. Constitution gives the executive branch and the president the power to appoint federal officials. Each of the following appointments requires the approval of the Senate:

- **Ambassadors**
- Federal judges
- Director of the FBI
- Heads of federal departments, such as the Department of Defense or the Department of Education

This photograph of the Senate chamber from 2010 shows the flag-draped coffin of Senator Robert Byrd. Byrd was the longest-serving member of Senate in U.S. history.

# CONGRESSIONAL DISTRICTS

A state's population determines the number of members it has in the House of Representatives. Each state has at least one representative in the House. Most states have more than one representative. These states are divided into congressional **districts**.

Each district elects one representative to the House. Each member of the House represents the people in that district. For example, California has 53 members in the House of Representatives. They come from 53 congressional districts.

## THE U.S. CENSUS

Every 10 years, the U.S. government takes a census. A census is a survey that collects data about people in the country. One of the main goals of the U.S. Census is to count the population of the states. This makes sure they're given the correct number of seats in the House of Representatives.

## GERRYMANDERING

Sometimes, congressional districts get redrawn to unfairly give one political party more power than another. This is called gerrymandering.

The word "gerrymander" comes from Elbridge Gerry. He approved the redrawing of congressional districts in the 1800s. People thought one of the new districts looked like a salamander. A cartoonist created a drawing of that district and called it a gerrymander.

# THE MAJORITY AND THE MINORITY

There are two big political parties in the United States. These are the Democratic and the Republican Parties. Each party has different opinions on issues like the environment, immigration, and taxes.

The party with more seats in each house of Congress is called the majority party. The other is called the minority party. Each party elects one of its members to be the party leader. Each party also has a position called a whip. The whip makes sure all the members vote the way the party wants them to.

In early 2020, the Republican Party is the majority party in the U.S. Senate. The majority leader is Mitch McConnell (right). The minority leader is Democrat Chuck Schumer (left).

# THE SPEAKER AND THE PRESIDENT PRO TEM

The leaders of the House of Representatives and the Senate aren't the same as the national party leaders. The Constitution states that the members of the House of Representatives must pick a Speaker of the House. The Speaker is the political leader of the House. They're part of the majority.

The leader of the Senate is the president pro tempore. This Latin phrase means "for the time being." This position is held by the longest-serving member of the majority party.

## RESPONSIBILITIES OF THE PRESIDENT PRO TEMPORE OF THE SENATE

- Leader of the Senate
- Communicates with the president of the United States
- Third in line to become president
- Schedules and organizes debates

# PRESIDENTIAL LINE OF SUCCESSION

1. VICE PRESIDENT

2. SPEAKER OF THE HOUSE

3. PRESIDENT PRO TEMPORE

4. SECRETARY OF STATE

This shows the line of succession for the presidency. These are the people who will lead the country if the president can't perform his or her duties.

## RESPONSIBILITIES OF THE SPEAKER OF THE HOUSE

- Leader of the House of Representatives
- Communicates with the president of the United States
- Official spokesperson of the House
- Second in line to become president
- Runs debates
- Determines when and how an issue will be debated
- Sets daily schedules
- Assigns bills to committees

# CONGRESSIONAL COMMITTEES

Most of the work done by Congress is split between committees. Each committee focuses on specific areas of interest or experience. For example, some focus on education or foreign relations.

Committees gather information to find **policy** problems. They come up with possible solutions. They then report to the other members of the chamber. Each committee is allowed to make its own rules about structure, organization, and **procedure**.

## TYPES OF CONGRESSIONAL COMMITTEES

There are three main types of congressional committees.

**Standing committees** are permanent committees that debate bills, monitor government agencies, and decide funding.

**Select or special committees** are made to study and investigate specific issues.

**Joint committees** are made up of members from both the Senate and the House of Representatives. Joint committees perform studies and address issues that concern both houses.

Congressional committees have their own meeting rooms. Committees meet in these rooms to discuss important issues.

# THE FILIBUSTER

There are rules for debate in Congress. Members of the House are allowed to speak for only a limited amount of time. In the Senate, members can speak for as long as they want. In fact, senators don't even have to talk about the issues they are debating.

Senators use this power in filibusters. This is when senators talk for a long time to stop or delay the Senate from voting on a bill or issue. The Senate can vote to end a filibuster. This is called a **cloture**.

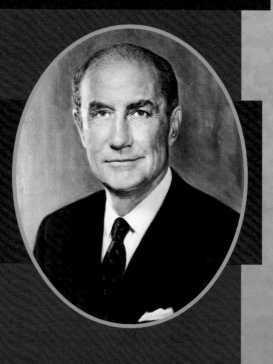

In 1957, Senator Strom Thurmond of South Carolina began a filibuster that became the longest filibuster to take place in the Senate since 1900.

Jeff Merkley, shown here at a press conference following his 2017 filibuster, spoke for 15 hours against the confirmation of Neil Gorsuch.

# MAKING LAWS

Congress was created to be the lawmaking branch of the government. A law starts as an idea proposed by a member of Congress. The idea becomes a bill, which is voted on by the members of each house. Both houses must agree on the exact same bill.

The bill is then sent to the president. If the president signs the bill, it becomes a law. If the president doesn't like the bill, they can **veto** it. This means they send it back to Congress.

### ✔ VERIFIED

This site has an updated list of how many laws each president has vetoed:
**https://history.house.gov/Institution/ Presidential-Vetoes/Presidential-Vetoes**

# HOW A BILL BECOMES A LAW

**I.** A member of Congress introduces a bill.

**2.** The bill is sent to one or more committees.

**3.** The bill is reviewed and discussed by members of the committee.

**4.** Changes may be made to the bill by members of the committee.

**5.** The bill is reviewed and discussed by members of the committee.

**6.** If the bill passess the vote in the first house, it's sent to the second house and the process begins again.

**7.** If the bill passes the vote in both houses, it's sent to the president.

**8.** The president can either sign the bill or veto the bill. Signing the bill makes it a law.

**9.** A vetoed bill goes back to Congress.

**10.** Congress can change the bill and start the process all over again, or it can vote to reject the president's veto and make the bill a law anyway.

The president has 10 days to sign or veto a bill sent to them by Congress. If they do nothing, the bill doesn't become a law. This is called a pocket veto.

# TAXES AND BUDGETS

Congress is allowed to raise taxes. It can also spend public money for government purposes. This is sometimes called the power of the **purse**. Article I of the U.S. Constitution gives the House of Representatives the power to create bills that raise money for the government.

Congress also passes the federal budget. The federal budget outlines all of the money the government will spend during the year.

# PASSING A FEDERAL BUDGET

**I.** The president sends a budget request to Congress.

**2.** Each house of Congress writes its own spending plan.

**3.** The House and Senate create bills that provide money to each government program.

**4.** Both houses meet to go over differences in their bills.

**5.** The budget is sent to the president and must be signed before becoming law.

The power to tax was given to the House of Representatives because the Founding Fathers believed that members of the House were more closely connected to the public.

# DECLARATION OF WAR

The U.S. Constitution gives Congress many military powers. It's in charge of war and defense. Congress has the power to create and **maintain** a national military. This includes an army and a navy.

Congress must also create a set of rules that the military follows. One of the most important powers given to Congress is the power to declare war. Under the Constitution, only Congress has the power to officially declare war.

## THE FIVE OFFICIAL WARS

The Constitution is unclear about how Congress is supposed to declare a war. The United States has fought in many wars, but only five have been officially declared by Congress. These were:

- The War of 1812 (1812–1815)

- The Mexican-American War (1846–1848)

- The Spanish-American War (1898)

- World War I (1914–1918)

- World War II (1939–1945)

# LETTERS OF MARQUE

One of the most unusual things Congress can do is issue letters of marque and reprisal. This means Congress has the power to hire private ship captains to attack or steal from enemy nations.

President Franklin D. Roosevelt gave a speech before both houses of Congress asking them to declare war on Japan following the attack on Pearl Harbor.

# TRADE, COMMERCE, AND COINS

There's a part of the Consitution called the commerce clause. It gives Congress the power to control trade between the states. It's also in charge of trade between the United States and other countries.

The Constitution also gives Congress the power to mint, or produce, money. Congress can control the value of money. It's also allowed to borrow money from other countries.

## OTHER POWERS OF CONGRESS

- The power to create the process that allows someone to become a citizen.

- The power to create post offices and to build roads to connect them.

- The power to set up a system of patents and copyrights.

- The power to set up a national capital.

The Founding Fathers made sure that the Constitution granted Congress the ability to create a process for immigrants to become citizens.

Congress can create laws that deal with bankruptcy. Bankruptcy helps people and businesses with **debt**.

# CONFIRMATION OF APPOINTEES

The Constitution created three different branches of government. The Founding Fathers were worried about one branch becoming too powerful. The Constitution gives each branch some powers. Other branches get other powers. This means they all check and balance each other.

For example, the president can appoint people to fill certain government positions. They can appoint heads of government agencies, ambassadors to foreign countries, or Supreme Court justices. All of these **appointees** must be confirmed by the Senate before they are allowed to fill that position. The Senate balances this power.

Because Supreme Court justices serve for life, appointing someone to the Supreme Court is one of the most important decisions that a president can make.

# IMPEACHMENT

    The term "impeachment" has been in the news a lot. Impeachment is one of the special powers given to Congress by the Constitution. Impeachment is a two-part process.

    The House of Representatives is allowed to investigate government officials. This includes the president and vice president. If the House thinks a serious crime has been committed, they can vote to impeach. An impeachment is an official criminal charge. After the House impeaches a government official, it's the Senate's job to hold a trial.

Although he was under investigation for his role in the Watergate scandal, President Richard Nixon resigned from office before he was impeached.

# THREE IMPEACHMENTS

Only three U.S. presidents have ever been impeached. None of these three were found guilty by the Senate or removed from office. They are:

## ANDREW JOHNSON
### (1865–1869)

Impeached for illegally firing and replacing the U.S. secretary of war

## BILL CLINTON
### (1993–2001)

Impeached for lying to federal investigators and for interfering in a criminal investigation

## DONALD TRUMP
### (2017–)

Impeached for abuse of power and for interfering in a congressional investigation

# REPRESENTATION FOR ALL

Congress is the branch of the U.S. government that most directly represents the American people. Senators and representatives are elected directly by the people they represent. The House and the Senate each have a lot of responsibilities. Voters think their representatives should understand them. There are people of many races, religions, and sexual orientations in the United States. Most believe Congress should represent all these groups.

Recent years have seen more people from minority groups elected to Congress. Fewer **candidates** backed by big businesses are getting elected. More voters support candidates who rely on smaller donations from the people they want to represent. Today's Congress is more diverse than ever. Voters think this will make Congress use its powers wisely.

Alexandria Ocasio-Cortez made headlines in 2018 when she was elected to the House of Representatives.

# GLOSSARY

**agency:** A government department that's responsible for a certain activity or area.

**ambassador:** An official representative or messenger, especially to another country.

**appointee:** A person chosen by the president to fill a position.

**candidate:** A person running for office.

**cloture:** The process used for ending a filibuster and taking a vote.

**debt:** Money owed to another.

**deny:** To refuse to accept.

**district:** An area created by the government for government business.

**establish:** To create something.

**federal:** Relating to the central government of the United States.

**independent:** Not controlled or ruled by another.

**maintain:** To keep something up.

**official:** A person who has a position of authority in the government.

**policy:** A law that people use to help them make decisions.

**procedure:** A series of steps followed in a set order.

**propose:** To suggest to a person or group of people to consider.

**purse:** An amount of money that the government can use.

**term:** The length of time for which a person holds a political office.

**veto:** To refuse to allow a bill to become a law.

# INDEX